ANIMAL RIGHTS

Designed and produced by
Aladdin Books Ltd
70 Old Compton Street
London W1

First published in the
United States in 1987 by
Gloucester Press
387 Park Avenue South
New York NY 10016

ISBN 0-531-170 45-4

Library of Congress Catalog
Card Number: 86-83111

Printed in Belgium

The front cover photograph shows a chimpanzee at the London Zoo.
The back cover photograph shows a bullfight, one of the most
controversial blood sports.

*The author, Miles Barton, has worked as an academic researcher on
animal welfare. He is a radio producer at the BBC's Natural History
Unit, Bristol, UK.*

Contents

Animal rights	4
Experimental tools?	6
Beauty and the beast	8
Profile: Laboratory animals	10
Cost of a conscience	12
Profile: Farm animals	14
On the move	16
Slaughter	18
Blood sports	20
Profile: The hunted	22
Fur trade	24
Man's best friends?	26
Changing attitudes	28
Hard facts	30
Useful addresses	31
Index	32

SURVIVAL · SURVIVAL · SURVIVAL

ANIMAL RIGHTS

Miles Barton

Gloucester Press

New York : Toronto : 1987

Animal rights

Humans have always exploited animals. They have hunted them for food and sport and harnessed them for power and transportation. In the past, there was little concern for the welfare of animals – except for where it related to their value as beasts of labor. This view is still held in parts of the world but attitudes are changing.

Today, many people are concerned about the welfare of animals in the wild, on farms, in zoos, in laboratories and even in the home. The first animal welfare organization was formed 160 years ago, but it is only in the last 10 years that the idea that animals have rights has gained acceptance in Europe, the United States and Australia.

Groups such as the extreme animal liberationists believe that animals have the right to an independent existence from humans. They claim that using animals for our convenience can never be justified. Some groups are prepared to kill, injure and destroy the property of those involved in what they consider to be animal abuse. Most people, however, consider we do have the right to use animals to meet human needs.

Whatever the conclusions of the debate, concern over the way we treat animals has never been greater. This book is about the use and abuse of animals by mankind and the rights of animals to better conditions wherever possible.

The photograph shows a peaceful demonstration against the use of animals in scientific research, London, UK. It is estimated that every six seconds, a laboratory animal dies in the UK.

Experimental tools?

Vivisection is the most controversial issue of animal rights. Vivisection means "cutting a living thing," but the word is commonly used to describe any experiment carried out on a live animal for scientific research. Millions of animals are used for research into heart disease, cancer and transplant techniques. In the United States alone, an estimated 65 million animals are used each year.

Most experiments are performed on rats and mice. Research with larger animals such as dogs and monkeys is more controversial. It is now accepted that these animals can suffer distress and, in most countries, laws restrict their use in laboratory experiments.

▽ A monkey was forced to inhale cigarettes to investigate the effects of smoking on health. Anti vivisectionists criticize these types of experiments. Humans do not need to smoke, they argue, therefore the pain and discomfort to the animal cannot be justified.

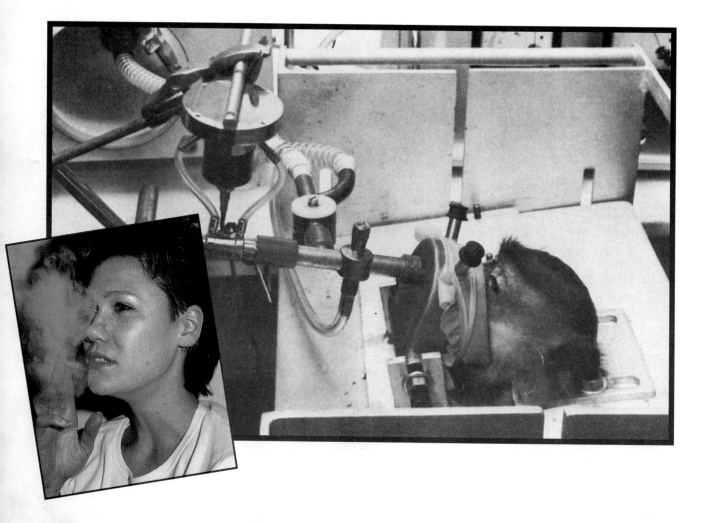

> "If the rat does not substitute for Man, then Man must become the guinea pig."
>
> Chemical Industries Association Ltd.

In some countries, scientists are compelled by law to weigh up the pain to the animal against the benefit to mankind. But is this always possible? Researchers say that it is often difficult to predict the exact benefits of a particular experiment, while animal liberationists believe that it is impossible to justify *any* experimentation on animals. But the numbers of animals used in research could be reduced by better communication among scientists to avoid the repetition of experiments.

▽ Experimental surgery on dogs has led to greatly improved surgery in the treatment of heart disease – one of the major causes of death in the West today. This is just one example of an animal experiment which has directly improved human life.

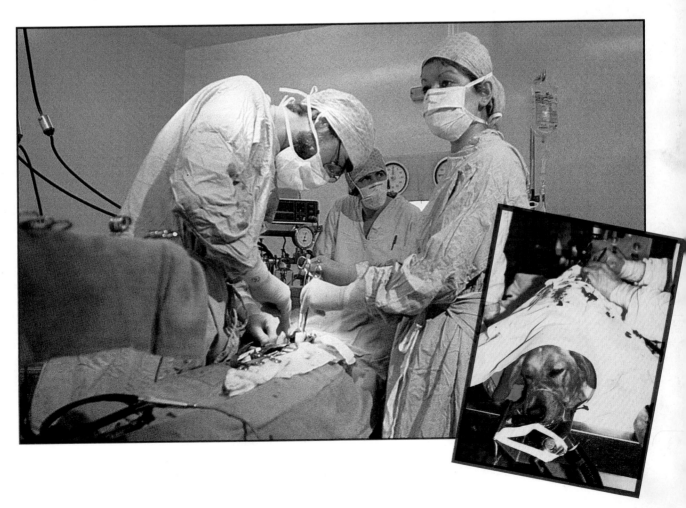

Beauty and the beast

In many countries, companies are compelled by law to test all new chemical products on animals. Lipsticks, toothpastes, shampoos and weedkillers undergo extensive testing to assess their potential side-effects on humans. Some of these tests have been criticized by scientists, either for being unreliable when their results are applied to humans, or because they use unnecessarily large numbers of animals. The LD50 test is especially criticized for these reasons. LD stands for lethal dose and in the experiment a chemical is injected in increasing amounts until 50 per cent of the animals die.

Increasingly, consumers are choosing products which have not been tested on animals. This has led some manufacturers to investigate alternative testing techniques. However, the use of animals for testing cosmetics and other non-medical products accounts for only a small proportion of animal experiments.

The Draize test (shown right), in which the chemical is dropped into the eye of a rabbit, is routinely used to test shampoos. Scientists are trying to find alternative testing methods, for example the use of cell cultures (cells from animals kept outside the body), and the use of computer models. But so far, the Draize test has not been successfully replaced.

Testing on animals
The diagram shows the percentage of different types of research which use animals. The majority of experiments are in the fields of medical and veterinary research and have led to improvements in the quality of life for *both* people and animals. Only a small proportion of animal experiments involve the testing of cosmetics. However, many people argue that there are plenty of cosmetics and shampoos on the market and that the testing of new products involves unnecessary suffering.

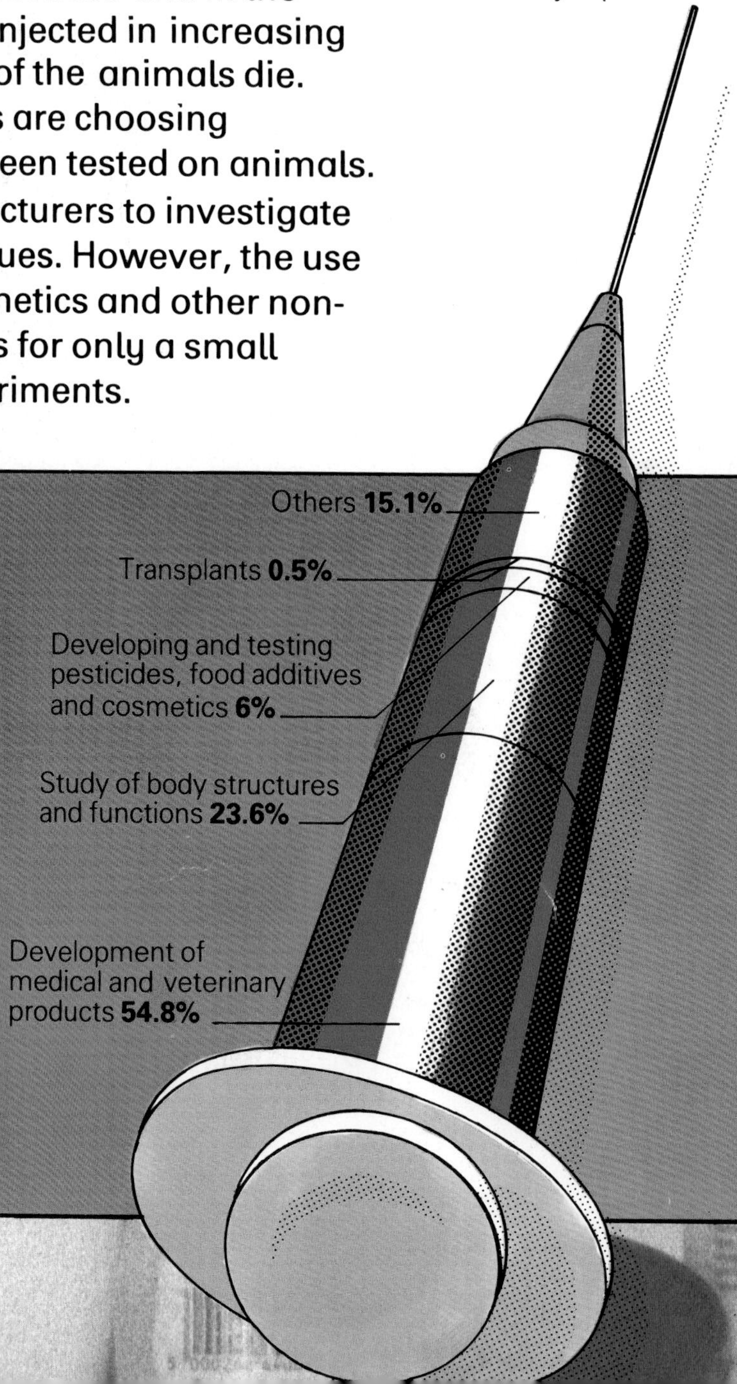

Others **15.1%**

Transplants **0.5%**

Developing and testing pesticides, food additives and cosmetics **6%**

Study of body structures and functions **23.6%**

Development of medical and veterinary products **54.8%**

Laboratory animals

Experimental animals range from chimpanzees to mice and rats specially bred for the purpose. Providing domesticated mice and rats with all they require is a relatively easy matter – even in the laboratory. Keeping a monkey or an ape healthy and contented is more difficult. However, since primates are the closest animals to man, they are used in many areas of research.

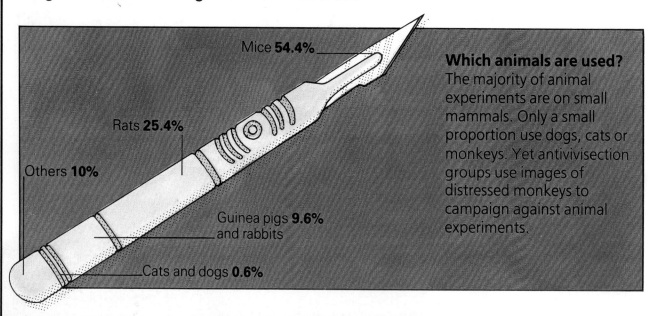

Mice **54.4%**

Rats **25.4%**

Others **10%**

Guinea pigs **9.6%** and rabbits

Cats and dogs **0.6%**

Which animals are used?
The majority of animal experiments are on small mammals. Only a small proportion use dogs, cats or monkeys. Yet antivivisection groups use images of distressed monkeys to campaign against animal experiments.

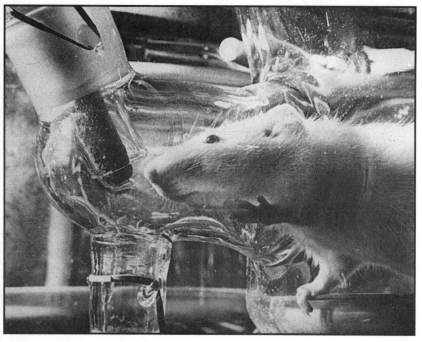

◁ **The rat**
The rat is the commonest laboratory animal after the mouse and is bred for research. Because of its intelligence, it is widely used in psychological experiments: it has been taught to find its way around mazes and to perform complex tasks for food rewards. Rats learn more quickly when given toys to play with than when kept in bare, empty cages. The photograph shows rats used in an experiment testing the effects of smoking.

▷ The macaque monkey

Several species of macaque are used in research. In some establishments they are bred in large outdoor cages, but many thousands are still imported from the Philippines and other parts of Asia each year. In the laboratory they are housed in metal cages either singly or in groups. Macaque monkeys have been used in the development of new drugs for treating epilepsy. Other experiments on the workings of the brain using these animals have been criticized.

▽ The chimpanzee

There are 1,200 chimpanzees currently held in research establishments throughout the world. Despite being an endangered species, chimps are usually caught in the wild because they are difficult to breed in captivity. The arrival of the disease AIDS could lead to an increase in their use as it affects them in a very similar way to humans. A European pharmaceuticals company was recently found to be keeping chimps in cages too small for them to stand upright, causing unnecessary stress.

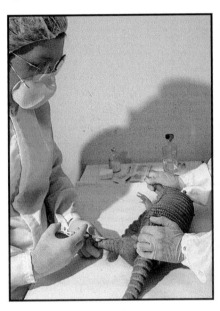

△ The armadillo

After humans, this is the next largest mammal to contract leprosy. For this reason it is now used to produce a vaccine against the disease which infects 15 million people worldwide. As many as 750 doses can be produced from the organs of one animal and armadillos are now being specially bred for this purpose.

Cost of a conscience

In recent years there has been a public outcry against factory farming – intensive farming methods which involve raising the largest number of animals on the smallest area of land. Factory farming uses modern farming methods to produce cheaper meat, milk and eggs.

"Consumers should have the choice to buy produce farmed extensively or intensively."

National Consumer Council, UK.

One of the main objections to intensive farming is that it forces animals to live in conditions which impose inhumane restrictions on the animals' behavior. Some countries in Europe have introduced legislation to ensure farmers provide their animals with less confined living conditions. This has led to some changes: for example, many farmers now rear veal calves in straw-covered yards instead of in crates.

Keeping chickens in battery cages has also been criticized. Many supermarkets now sell eggs from free-range chickens as well as from battery hens, thus giving the consumer a choice. But is everyone prepared to pay the extra 10-30 per cent which free-range farming costs?

Cheap meat in the butcher's shop is often paid for by the suffering of the animals. But some butchers now give consumers a choice by also selling meat from animals which have not been intensively farmed. Vegetarians consider eating meat can never be justified, no matter how the animals are reared.

△ Battery hens are kept four to a cage, unable to stretch their wings. In some parts of Europe these cages are now being made illegal.
▽ In France, geese and ducks are force-fed with vast quantities of salty corn. This causes their livers to swell to several times their normal size. After weeks, or even months, of force-feeding, the birds are killed and the livers used to produce a highly prized paté.

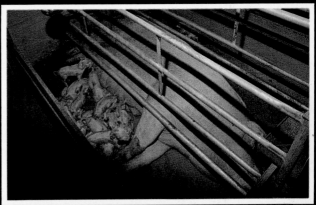

△ Pigs are kept in buildings where temperature, lighting and feed can be easily controlled so as to fatten quickly.
▽ Many veal calves are still reared in small crates. They are only fed on milk and kept in darkness for up to six months, and then slaughtered.

SURVIVAL **PROFILE...**

Farm animals

Because farm animals are reared to provide us with food and clothing, we regard them in a different way from other animals and our concern for their welfare tends to be less. However, most farmers realize they have a strong interest in the well-being of their stock: ill-treated animals produce poor quality meat.

▷ **Domestic fowl**
Free-range hens scratch for feed in the farmyard. Critics of factory farming argue that it is more humane to keep chickens in this way. However, battery hens kept in artificially-lit sheds are freer from disease. They can also produce eggs all year round and in greater quantity than free-range hens. Chickens and eggs provide a cheap source of food in the West and many cannot afford to pay the higher prices that free-range farming bring.

◁ **Domestic cow**
The photograph shows a two-hour-old calf with its mother. Cows usually give birth to one calf per year but it is often removed from the mother within the first week of life, so that we can have the milk. Cows can live up to 12 years of age, but once their milk yield drops, at about seven years of age, they are usually sent for slaughter. Dairy and beef cattle are often housed and fed indoors during the winter months.

▷ Sheep

The photograph shows a farmer tending sheep in Australia where sheep farming is a major part of the economy. The sheep are kept on large farms and in some cases are only rounded up for shearing. This means that many animals suffer neglect on the farm; eight million die each year from disease and starvation and many more die if there is a drought. Twenty per cent of the lambs die before they are two months old. Supporters of intensive farming methods point to situations like these as examples of how huge numbers of animals cannot be managed properly under extensive farming systems. They claim that disease and mortality can be better controlled under intensive farming systems.

◁ Oxen

In Asia and parts of Africa, oxen like these are used to plow the fields. Not only do these domestic animals serve as beasts of burden, but they can also be milked, their calves slaughtered, and, at the end of their working lives, they provide meat and hide.

On the move

The transporting of animals over long distances by road, sea and air is now a major cause of concern to animal welfare groups. Wild animals caught in the tropics of South America, Africa and the Far East are brought to Europe and the United States for the pet trade. Consignments of birds and reptiles are often brought in by air but many do not survive the journey.

Domestic animals are also transported long distances: cattle and sheep may be bought and sold several times in their lives to exploit different pastures or changes in market prices.

Sometimes animals destined for slaughter are exported live to save on refrigeration and packing costs. Seven million live sheep are sent each year from Australia to the Middle East. Usually, it is the animals with the least commercial value that suffer most. For example, chickens are tightly packed in crates and many die from suffocation or exposure in transit.

▷ The main photograph shows how exotic birds are packed in containers ready for illegal shipment to Europe, where they will be smuggled through customs and sold illegally either privately or in pet shops. The inset photograph shows the fate of 2,000 birds (finches, parakeets and mynah birds) which did not survive the flight from India to the UK.

▽ In western Australia sheep are moved long distances in road-train transporters. Many do not survive the journey.

Slaughter

◁ The photograph shows the electrical stunning of a sheep immediately before slaughter. In many countries, stunning is required by law – but exceptions are allowed. Both Jewish and Islamic laws forbid the eating of animals damaged in any way before the act of slaughter. But, it is argued, extremely sharp knives are used, so that the animals feel no pain. However, scientists believe that animals may show signs of consciousness for nearly a minute after the cut. Humane societies are campaigning for an end to these methods of slaughter without stunning.

Since most of us regularly eat meat, millions of animals are slaughtered every day. Many countries have laws that control how and where slaughter can take place, but the methods of slaughter are still very controversial.

In a modern slaughterhouse, cattle are driven along a narrow passageway to a stunning box. This is a crate in which the animal is stunned, often by a "captive bolt" – a bullet which strikes the animal's skull. The side of the box then opens and the animal rolls out. It is then hoisted by the hind legs and its throat is cut by hand with a knife. Sheep are also killed in this way but they may be stunned by an electric shock instead.

New, more humane methods of slaughter are still being researched. Some animal welfare organizations recommend the use of carbon dioxide gas which puts the animal to sleep. They also recommend the use of cushioned conveyor systems which take the animals to the stunning point automatically.

▷ Sheep are usually electrically stunned and shackled upside down on a moving hoist. However, some studies have shown that over 30 per cent of the animals are still conscious when their throats are cut and electrical stunning is increasingly criticized as unreliable. Research shows that animals which are distressed at the time of slaughter produce meat of a reduced quality.

Blood sports

Blood sports have always been popular and in some countries they are an important part of the people's tradition and culture. Falconry and deer hunting go back thousands of years while fox hunting and hare coursing began much more recently. Shooting as a sport is widely practiced throughout Europe and North America — thousands of pigeons, pheasants and ducks are shot each year.

Animal welfare groups argue that blood sports should be banned. They also say that hunting with hounds is worse than shooting because of the distress caused by the chase. The hunters, however, claim their sport is justified as the culling, reducing the numbers, of species such as deer and foxes is necessary; people have removed the animals' natural predators and provided them with extra food through farming. They also point out that large areas of land have been preserved for wildlife because of hunting.

▷ Every year thousands of bulls and hundreds of horses are killed or maimed in Spanish bullrings and in the arenas of France, Portugal, Mexico and South America. In Spain alone bullfighting is estimated to be a $100 million industry and has great cultural importance. But does this justify the continued and persistent infliction of pain on an animal for the pleasure of the spectators?

▷ In Europe and North America there has recently been an upsurge in illegal dog-fighting, badger-baiting and raccoon-baiting. Bull terriers are placed in rings with another dog, or a badger, to fight to death while spectators bet heavily on the winner. Sports like cock-fighting (far right) which involve pitting one animal against another are also banned in much of the West — but they are still very popular in the Far East and Mexico.

SURVIVAL PROFILE...

The hunted

Many biologists and conservationists now say that some forms of hunting can benefit an animal population. In parts of Africa, hunters from the United States and Europe pay large amounts of money to shoot individual elephants or lions. Only a few animals are shot for trophies and so the population remains higher than if the land were given over to agriculture. Similar situations occur with deer, boar and pheasant in Europe and in North America.

◁ **The boar**
In the last 50 years boar hunting has become a popular sport in France. Large estates are set aside for boar where gamekeepers control predators and may even feed the boar during bad winters. Boar may be hunted with hounds on horseback, the animal being finally killed by a hunter with a short sword. Sometimes they are driven into the open by beating the undergrowth and shot by waiting hunters.

◁ The fox

The fox has been hunted in Britain with hounds for the last 250 years. It has long been argued that the fox kills domestic animals such as lambs and chickens and that hunting is a fair means of control. Yet some scientists suggest that foxes rarely take live lambs, preferring to scavenge for food. The killing of the fox by hounds, although quick, must be painful. Further cruelty may be involved if a terrier is used to drive the fox from its earth.

△ The deer

Deer can be hunted on horseback with hounds, which surround the deer and prevent its escape, or by stalking and shooting. Deerstalking has become a profitable industry and popular in the United States. Deer stocks are carefully managed so that the shooting is part of a culling program to maintain the population at a level the land can support.

The passenger pigeon

This is the most famous case of animal extermination due to hunting. During the last century passenger pigeons were an extremely successful species of bird – some estimates claim they made up 40 per cent of the entire bird population of North America. However, their numbers diminished rapidly because of shooting. In 1900, the last passenger pigeon seen in the wild was shot down in Ohio.

Fur trade

The fur trade has been vigorously attacked by the animal welfare and animal rights groups. They argue that because fur now tends to be a luxury product, with man-made alternatives easily available, the trade is outdated, barbaric and unnecessary.

The United States traps more animals than any other country except the USSR. These include wolves, muskrats, beavers, mink and even weasels.

△ Fur coats are a symbol of luxury. Many countries now ban fur trade in jaguar, leopard, tiger and ocelot.

◁ American minks are kept singly in cages with a nest box attached. Mating is carried out in March with an average litter of five kittens arriving in May. They are weaned in June and killed in December when the fur is at its best.

△ Animals, such as this tiger which is an endangered species, may be caught accidentally by traps. Once trapped, the animal faces hours, or even days of pain; some animals will gnaw their legs off to escape the grip of the trap. Many countries have now banned the use of these traps but the major fur traders, the USA and the USSR, continue to use them to trap a wide variety of small animals such as beaver and muskrat.

Both professional and part-time hunters set traps in the wilds of North America. They say that this allows for the harvesting or culling of animals which would otherwise become pests. Conservationists point out that traps kill indiscriminately and may often trap the wrong species, including birds protected by law.

Most minks used for fur are now ranched rather than caught in the wild. As forty to sixty animals are required to make one fur coat, great numbers of animals are raised worldwide. Fur breeders argue that farming is preferable to trapping because the quality of the fur can be controlled. They also claim that farming is less cruel as the animals are killed painlessly.

Man's best friends?

At first sight, the devoted pet on the hearth may not appear to be of concern to animal welfare groups. Yet many people thoughtlessly mistreat their pets by overfeeding or under-exercising them. Exotic pets, which are often imported illegally, are even more likely to be mistreated. Monkeys or wild cats are kept as status symbols, but they suffer in close confinement. Snakes and alligators may be sold to owners who do not know how to look after these animals properly. Once the owners realize these animals make unsuitable pets, they may be abandoned.

Animal liberationists argue that no animal should be confined, not even a cat or a dog. Circuses are the main targets for their criticism because, they say, they exploit animals solely for our entertainment. However, most circus owners claim that their animals are kept in good condition and that the animals enjoy performing.

▽ Every year thousands of people flock to the Big Top for the glamor and excitement which the circus offers. But now that television has brought the natural behavior of animals into the home, animal welfare groups are saying that the entertainment provided by performing animals is cruel, degrading and unnecessary.

Children often tease their pets and, without realizing, cause them suffering. Pets also suffer deliberate ill-treatment. Thousands of puppies and kittens are abandoned each year (main photograph). In the United States, about 7.6 million unwanted pets were destroyed in 1985. It has been estimated that one-third of the American dog population ends up in animal shelters.

27

Changing attitudes

Attitudes to animals have changed in the last 100 years, and today many societies have a greater respect for animal welfare. For example, concern about experiments with live animals has led to changes in the law. In the UK, since 1987, each scientific project using animals has to be registered to ensure that animals are used only in approved experiments.

Other important changes in animal welfare have been achieved by economic means. The switch to veal calves reared in straw yards and the decline of the Canadian baby seal cull were both brought about by the refusal of individuals and governments to buy products which involved unnecessary suffering to animals.

As individuals we can all improve the lives of animals by becoming more concerned about the way we treat them. And by knowing more about the pets we keep, we can ensure they live in the best conditions.

▽ As the human population expands there is less and less room for wildlife. The preservation of wild animals can only be achieved if people become aware of their importance and needs. Although regarded as prisons by the animal rights campaigners, many people believe that well-run zoos or parks will have a part to play in this education of the public.

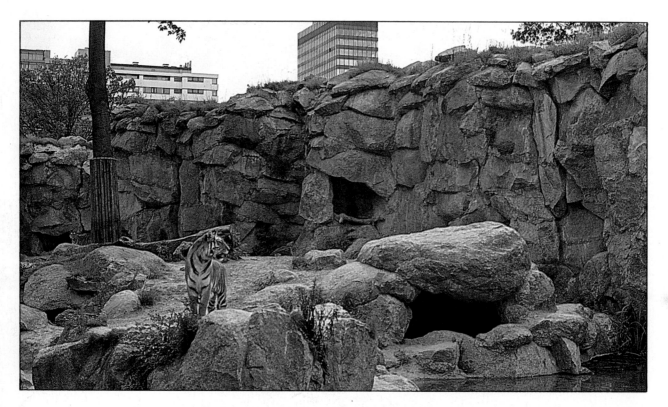

▷ In 1982, in response to
enormous public pressure, the
European Parliament banned
the importation of skins of
harp and hooded seal pups.
This reduced the kill in
Canadian waters from about
180,000 in the late 1970s to
only a few in 1986.

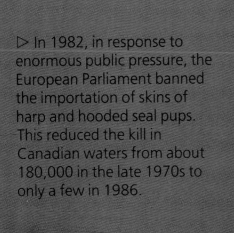

Hard facts

Listed below are those countries with laws controlling the use of animals in laboratories. Vivisection is worldwide but standards and conditions vary. Often, it is those countries where respect for animal welfare is strongest which have the most effective laws to control how animals are treated in laboratories.

Argentina
Both the experimenter and the institution have to be licensed.

Australia
No licensing or inspection requirements but local ethics committees examine experimental proposals to ensure they comply with a Code of Practice.

Austria
Licensing of institution and inspection by authorities is required. Unlicensed experimenters face six weeks' imprisonment. 500,000 animals are used each year.

Belgium
Every institution must be licensed. Cruelty and unnecessary mutilation of animals are punished by up to three months' imprisonment. 440,000 animals are used each year.

Canada
Scientists are subject to the guidelines of the Canadian Council on Animal Care.

Finland
Experimenter and institution must be licensed and inspected. Experiments are overseen by an ethical committee. 400,000 animals are used each year.

France
Licensing of experimenter and inspection is required by law.

Greece
The licensing of experiments is required but no inspection.

Holland
Each institution has to be licensed and inspected. Alternatives to animals are to be used where possible and lower animals are to be used in preference to higher. Offenses are punished by up to six months in prison.

Ireland
Every experimenter and institution has to be licensed.

Italy
Institutions are licensed and inspected. Offenses are punished by fines. 1.2 million animals are used each year.

Japan
There are no licensing laws, inspection or penalties.

Kenya
Each experimenter must be licensed and inspected. Offenses are punished by up to three months in prison.

Norway
Experimenters and institutions have to be licensed and inspected. 130,000 animals are used each year. Special permission is required for the use of dogs, cats, monkeys and apes.

Poland
Experimenters and institutions are licensed and are fined in the case of unnecessary cruelty. 100,000 animals are used each year.

Union of Soviet Socialist Republic
There are no licensing laws but some inspection is carried out by members of the Society for the Protection of Nature.

United Kingdom
Every experimenter and institution has to be licensed and inspected. Offenses are punished by up to six months' imprisonment. Only animals from certified breeding establishments can be used. 3.4 million animals were used in 1984.

United States of America
Every institution is registered and inspected. It is estimated that 65 million animals are used each year in research.

West Germany
Each institution is licensed and inspected. Unlicensed experimenters face up to two years' imprisonment.

Source: Universities' Federation for Animal Welfare, 1986, UK

The Animals' Agenda

magazine serves the international animal rights network as an independent "clearinghouse" for information on issues and activities. $18.00 for annual subscription, $2.00 sample copy.
P.O. Box 5234
Westport, CT 06881
203/226-8826

Farm Animal Reform Movement (FARM)

campaigns for humane farming practices, and also promotes vegetarianism.
P.O. Box 70123
Washington, D.C. 20088
301/530-1737

The Fund For Animals

Primarily a wildlife advocacy group which is well known for massive rescue operations and anti-fur campaigns.
200 W. 57th St.
New York, New York 10019
212/246-2096

Greenpeace

Mainly an environmental protection and wildlife conservation organization famous for confrontations with whaling vessels on the high seas.
1611 Connecticut Avenue, NW
Washington, D.C. 20070
202/462-1177

The Humane Society of the United States

A multi-issue animal protection organization, the largest in North America.
2100 L Street, NW
Washington, D.C. 20037
202/452-1100

The International Fund for Animal Welfare

Operates worldwide to stop cruelty to all animals, and to protect wild animal species from extinction.
P.O. Box 193
Yarmouth Port, MA 02675
617/362-4944

Index

A animal rights groups, 5, 7, 8, 16, 19, 20, 24, 26, 28, 31
animal shelters, 27
apes, 10, 30
armadillos, 11

B battery hens, 12, 13, 14
birds, 16, 17, 20, 22, 23
blood sports, 20, 21
breeders, 26, 30

C cages, 10, 11, 12, 13
cats, 10, 16, 30
cattle, 14, 16
chickens, 12, 13, 14, 16
chimpanzees, 10, 11
cigarette smoking, 6, 10
circuses, 26
conservationists, 22, 31
cosmetics, 8

D disease, 14, 15, 26
dogs, 6, 10, 16, 20, 26, 30
dolphins, 26
Draize test, 8, 9
drought, 15

E experiments, 6, 7, 8, 10, 11, 28, 30

F factory farming, 4, 12, 14, 28
force-feeding, 13
free-range farming, 12, 14
fur trade, 24, 25

G Greenpeace, 31
guinea pigs, 10

H human diseases, 7, 11
hunting, 20, 22, 23, 25

I intensive farming, 12, 13, 14, 15

J Jewish Law, 19

L laboratories, 4, 10, 11, 30
LD50 test, 8
legislation, 7, 8, 30

M malnutrition, 15, 26
medical research, 6, 7, 8, 10, 11
mice, 10
mink, 24, 25
monkeys, 6, 10, 11, 30

P parks, 28
passenger pigeon, 23

pet trade, 16, 26, 27
pets, 26, 27, 28

R rabbits, 8, 10
rats, 8, 10
research institutions, 11, 30

S scientific research, 5, 6, 7, 8, 10, 11
seal culling, 28, 29
sheep, 15, 16, 17, 19
slaughter, 16, 18, 19, 28
stress, 11
suffocation, 16

T transport, 16-17
traps, 24, 25

V veal calves, 12, 13, 28
vegetarians, 12, 31
veterinary research, 8
vivisection, 6, 8, 10, 11, 30

W welfare, 5, 14, 19, 20, 24, 26, 28, 31

Z zoos, 4, 26, 28

Photographic Credits:
Cover and pages 11, 13, 14, and 16: Robert Harding; pages 4-5: Roy Reed/Lawrence and Beavan; pages 6, 9, 10, 13, 17 (inset), 20-21, 23, 24, 27, 29 and 31: Scottish Society for the Prevention of Vivisection; pages 6, 9, 12-13 and 24: David West; pages 7, 23, 26 and 28: Spectrum; pages 7 and 11: Brian Gunn/ National Anti-Vivisection Society; pages 11, 17, 21, 22, 25, 29 and back cover: Bruce Colman; pages 13 and 14: Ardea; page 18: page 19: Lawrence and Beavan; page 27: Catherine Bradley.

PRINTED IN BELGIUM BY
proost
INTERNATIONAL BOOK PRODUCTION